Cuckoo Woo Woo

That Chick can Rock and Roll!

by Jennifer Daniels

Illustrations by John Goldacker

A companion book to
Jennifer Daniels' music album
It's Gonna Be A Good Day!

Listen while you read. Download the song for free at
JenniferDaniels.com.

We were delighted
to find you there,
a fuzzy chicken
with golden hair
who looked so worried,
shy, and trembling.

So your daddy's a Dodo,
and your mamma is Cuckoo.
You got Rooster in your soul,
and some Kookaburra too.

Don't you worry.
You'll have
all you need.

You twirled around till you found some space, and put a smile on your lovely face.

It took a while,
but it was not long.
You heard yourself
and you sang your song.

So your daddy's a Dodo,
and your mamma is Cuckoo.

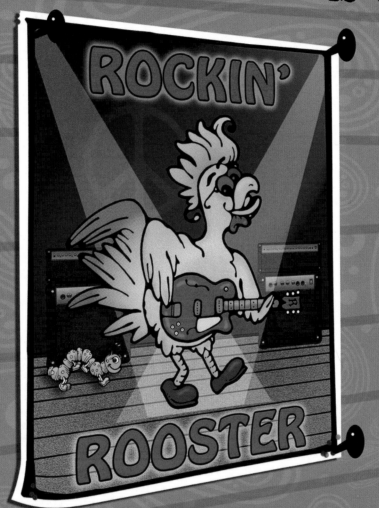

You got Rooster in your soul,
and some Kookaburra too.

hips shaking from
side to side says

A mommy bird with her wings out wide,

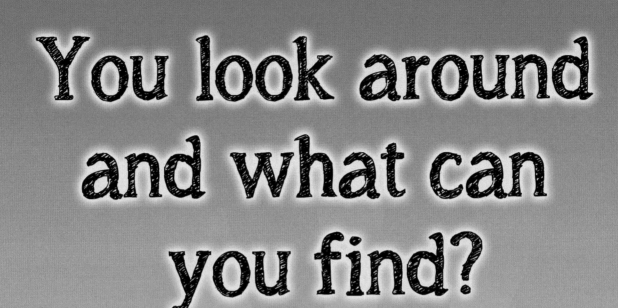

You look around and what can you find?

A bumblebee and a dandelion.

She said,
"Your daddy's a Dodo

and your mamma
is Cuckoo."

To my mom,
Carolyn Stooksbury Sunderland,
who is a force of God's provision,
as well as one hip granny bird.

And to Nancy Burton, a gifted teacher,
who allowed us to be "Cuckoo WooWoo."

Special thanks to
Mac McMullin, Tony and Marlene Neal,
Maxine and Pard Ward,
Larry Daniels, and Julie Stokes.

- Jennifer Daniels

Thank you Jennifer Daniels!

Dedicated to my mother Mona Jones,
grannies Elizabeth Goldacker, and Eva Smittle.
And my son's mother Jennifer English Goldacker.

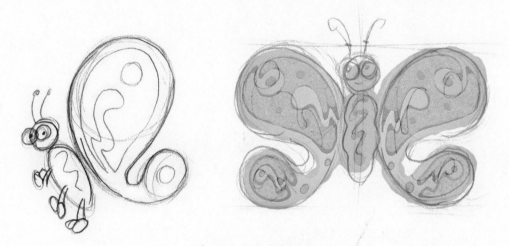

And to You.
You are All beautiful butterflies.

- John Goldacker

Cuckoo Woo Woo
That Chick can Rock and Roll!
by Jennifer Daniels
Illustrations by John Goldacker

visit: jenniferdaniels.com

Cuckoo Woo Woo
That Chick can Rock and Roll!
by Jennifer Daniels
Illustrations by John Goldacker

visit: jenniferdaniels.com

Jennifer Daniels, a writer and performer out of Lookout Mountain, Georgia, has been touring for twenty years, and has released seven albums with husband, guitar and mandolin player, Jeff Neal (and their old road hound, Bob Marley).

Eight years ago, they also released boy/girl twins, and this book, with it's companion music album, marks their first kids' project.

Jennifer and Jeff perform interactive kids' shows with an emphasis on literacy, and they offer a week-long school initiative called Songwriting IS Writing! The Write to Record for Literacy Project.

JenniferDaniels.com

Most of the artwork "Java" John Goldacker has created over the past 45 years has centered around his love of music, specifically Rock and Roll.

Also a life-long lover of children's books and cartoons, John illustrated the Florida legend, "River Dragon," and "Bud The Spud," a cautionary tale about a boy who turns into a couch potato!

javahnagila@hotmail.com

Made in the USA
Columbia, SC
27 July 2021